STOCK MARKET INVESTMENT FOR BEGINNERS

DISCLAIMER

Copyright © 2017

All Rights Reserved

No part of this book can be transmitted or reproduced in any form including print, electronic, photocopying, scanning, mechanical or recording without prior written permission from the author.

While the author has taken the utmost effort to ensure the accuracy of the written content, all readers are advised to follow information mentioned herein at their own risk. The author cannot be held responsible for any personal or commercial damage caused by information. All readers are encouraged to seek professional advice when needed.

BOOK DESCRIPTION

The stock markets are a collection of markets and exchange, where issuing and trading of equities of public listed companies, bonds. other securities through formal exchanges or over the counter markets. It involves buying and selling shares and securities to generate capital. The stock exchange market is what made Warren Buffet super rich. If you are able to monitor the situation of the securities and their patterns with time, you can truly make a fortune that can last you several lifetimes. This book aims at showing you how to take advantage of the stock exchange market and mint millions from the few thousand dollars stuffed under your mattress or that you have saved in the bank. The stock market was once thought to be a thing for the elite class but things have changed now. The stock exchange market is a great business opportunity for every citizen of planet earth.

The reason for companies trading their stocks is to generate enough capital to facilitate their business operations to a whole new level expanding their market reach and increasing profit income. As a prospective investor, you have to buy floating shares or stocks at a lower rate and hold onto them until the stocks experience a boom and their prices go up. At this point, you can sell your shares at a higher rate than you bought them making a considerable amount of profit. Some of the best investors in the stock market make millions of dollars from one trade! This book aims at making you wealthy and rich by trading in the stock market.

Contents

DISCLAIMER 2

BOOK DESCRIPTION 3

INTRODUCTION 7

WHAT IS A STOCK MARKET? 11

THE STOCK MARKET DO'S AND DON'TS 14

STOCK INVESTMENT SECTORS 20

MARKET CAPITALIZATION.. 27

STOCK ANALYSIS 31

GETTING STARTED 34

FREQUENTLY ASKED QUESTIONS 52

CONCLUSION 55

INTRODUCTION

A stock or share is a unit of ownership in a company. When bought the buyer becomes a shareholder to the company. This means that the shareholder is subjected to annual profit returns in terms of dividends. This is one advantage of dealing in shares; you have a regular income return in form of dividends after every financial year of the company. The amount of dividend you receive depend on the number of shares under your name. The more shares you buy, the more income you get. Shareholders do also have a limited contribution to the decision-making process in the company. The shareholders who own a large percentage of shares do have a lot of power when it comes to making decisions and their votes are very important. They are usually the controlling shareholders of the company. However, most companies are very careful when trading in the stock market, as they can lose control of the company to business people planning for a hostile takeover. This form of investment in shares is referred to as equity investment.

Stocks are one of the best investments to go for. This is because they have higher returns. However, they also do have higher risks as most markets are uncertain and cannot control the demand

and supply dynamics in them. It is thus advisable to spend big if you are quite certain of the potential of certain company shares in the stock market. The company share prices depend on the demand and supply of the goods and services offered by the companies listed in the stock market.

When the company is doing well and its products are in high demand, then the share price of the company increase. If the company is performing dismally and its products and services are low in demand, then the share price decreases. As a smart investor, you should scrutinize the factors causing the shift in market dynamics before purchasing a stock. It is important that you have a clear picture of what is before you. In most cases companies may experience a decrease in the share price because of new competitors or decline in product quality. However, you do know the potential of these companies and they will surely find a way back at the top. What do you do? You purchase the shares of these companies when they are at their lowest and hold on to them. In the meantime, you enjoy dividends until the company experiences a boom and they are back at the top and their share prices rocket. At this moment you sell the shares you bought at a higher price that will certainly give you enormous profit returns.

However, if the market factors are supreme and there is no way a company can overcome them, you should hold on to your money and avoid investing in such companies. This because the company may plunge into considerable debts and operate at a loss resulting in it being unlisted from the bourse or worse become insolvent. The investment in shares has become easier with the improvement of technology over the years. Today, everyone can afford a desktop or laptop and the various applications and algorithms developed to monitor the stock market dynamics. You can now buy or sell stock at the click of a mouse.

However, before you click that mouse consider reading this book first. The stock market is sometimes a scary and risky investment and can make you wealthy overnight or end up living in the streets. To succeed in this stock investment, you have to be smart, patient and sure of what you are doing. This is the main reason for writing this book, to equip you with these tools of success. In this century, people who work smart end up at the top. People who work smart accumulate enormous wealth that leaves others wondering how they pulled that off.

Ever heard of Ron Wayne, he is the other founder of Apple Inc, apart from Steve Job and Steve Wozniak. He sold his shares at $800 but had he not sold the shares, the shares would have had an estimated value of $35 billion dollars today. Maybe he had other plans of his own, but surely he must regret this move now and then. Thus to avoid making choices that might deny you the chance of living a billionaire's life, read this book. It will show you how to accumulate wealth by trading in the stock market. Most importantly it will make you a Warren Buffet, knowing which stocks to buy and which not to.

WHAT IS A STOCK MARKET?

A stock market is a system where shares, derivatives, options and similar financial instruments from different companies are issued, bought, and then sold.

All across the world, there are stock markets where millions of stocks from hundreds of companies are traded on a daily basis. There is a lot of speculation in the stock market. There are investors who buy shares of a company, in the hopes that it will perform well in the future. There are also investors who sell shares of a company when they believe that the company will perform poorly in the future or if this is the best time to cash out on the gains.

DIFFERENT TYPES OF STOCKS

Before you trade, you need to know the types of stocks and be able to identify them when you see them. Each kind of stock has its own uniqueness, advantages, and disadvantages. You need to match each kind of stock with the investment strategy that fits it and your risk capabilities. i.e. do you want to be more speculative or play it safe at the cost of fewer returns?

1) **Blue Chip Stock** - This is a stock that is considered safer compared to other stocks. Blue chip companies are typically well established in their field and enjoy favorable financial conditions. They also pay dividends on a more standard schedule. They are the large cap companies. While they are generally considered safe if the market falls they tend to follow. These stocks are what you would add to a portfolio to mitigate risks.

2) **Preferred Stock** - This is a type of ownership of a stock that has a mix of stock and bond characteristics. It offers fixed dividends, as well as price appreciation. It differs from traditional stocks as traditional stocks don't offer fixed dividends, only occasional dividends. Preferred stocks, however, don't appreciate as well as traditional stocks, but preferred stock-holders will be paid before common stock holders in the event the company is liquidated.

3) **Dividend Stock** - Just as the name suggests, these are stocks of companies that generally pay out dividends. Not all stocks pay out dividends. In fact, many don't. These stocks generally pay out increasing dividends each year. They differ from traditional stocks since their dividends aren't fixed or guaranteed.

4) **Penny Stock** - This is a high risk, low-priced stock that is typically shunned by the general investing crowd, except for those who really know what they're doing. Technically, stocks that trade at a price of $5 per share or lower are considered

penny stocks. These are stocks of companies that would be considered risky but have great yields IF it works out. They might be unestablished or poorly performing companies. One of the main drawbacks of these stocks, aside from the risk, is that they are not very liquid. This means that if you want to sell your shares, you might have a hard time finding buyers right away. Or you will have to sell them at a huge loss.

5) **Growth Stock** - These are stocks of companies with earnings that are expected to increase, compared to the general stock market. These stocks typically don't pay dividends. Instead of paying dividends, a company will spend their extra profits on reinvesting the money back into the company, so they can continue to grow. Earnings refer to revenue minus expenses for a company.

6) **Value stock** - These are stocks that trade lower than their perceived value. These stocks generally pay dividends and are found by the use of fundamental analysis techniques, which we will get into soon.

THE STOCK MARKET DO'S AND DON'TS

Helpful tips before you invest in stock exchange markets:

THE DO'S

1) Be Patient and Optimistic - The stock market is always fluctuating. You usually don't have a continuous increase or decrease without some ups and downs. This is why even as a beginner, you need to stick with the investment. This can be hard right in the beginning. You are excited to make a lot of money and may feel like you aren't earning fast enough. Some people aren't willing to stick for ten years or more with one stock in the hopes of earning some good money. But if you want to really make good money with this investment, you need to get into the stock market now and stay with it for the long term. This is when the best returns come into play.

2) Have a better understanding of your current financial standings - This helps you to know how much you own and owe. It also helps you to know how much money you have free for investment. Determining your financial standing involves creating a personal financial statement. The financial statement has been discussed later in this book. Don't over commit funds you can't afford to be tied up in stock investments. Stocks are medium to long term investment instruments after all.

3) Put your money together - Make sure you have more than enough money in reserve. Make sure there is an emergency fund you can fall on. List your assets in order of liquidity so you can determine the assets you can easily convert into cash if you run out of capital.

4) Determine your risk level - You have to know how much you are willing to lose if things don't go the way you want. It is wise to create red flags at thresholds. If the market falls to a particular point that you are not willing to go beyond? Sell your stocks, even if you have made a loss. Taking a risk beyond your capacity can be dangerous. Resist the temptation to hold on to failing stocks. Although it may rebound in the future?

5) Research and study the market well – We will repeat this over and over again, great understanding of the market is number one priority. You need to be able to study the market very carefully, no shortcuts and form a trend over a period of time. Trends are usually influenced by market indicators. Study these indicators to know the cause of the trend you are seeing in the market. For instance, if the S & P 500 keeps increasing steadily, it means market capitalization is getting bigger and the market is in a bullish period.

But you need to know the particular companies to invest in. Study the industries and pick an industry that is performing well. Check out the biggest losers and gainers in the industry. Pick out a few companies and concentrate on them. Study these companies and their owners and decide whether they are big or small company (based on the cap), stable or unstable (based on internal and external events).

6) Determine your investment strategy - Your investment strategy will determine your approach to investing. Once you know your risk factors and you understand the market, you can follow the investment strategy that suits your goals. Do you want to go through companies' statement of accounts and select stocks that trade for less than their actual value (fundamental) or you would rather go through the stock's chart and find short term trading opportunities(technical trading)? Or have you come across a special and significant piece of information you know will greatly impact share prices? There are many factors in decision making with stocks.

THE DON'TS

1) Do not get attached to a particular stock - Do not get emotionally attached to a particular stock. While being an emotional venture, stocks investments should not be controlled by emotions. Don't attach sentimental value to any stock. The best investments may do well for a long while, and accrue considerable wealth, but every stock has its nadir, and the best investors also know when it is time to cash out.

2) Chasing a losing stock - As stated earlier in the book, you need to have a threshold for loss; the amount of money you can afford to lose. Also, don't buy a losing stock. When you've seen a stock deteriorate steadily and you can't point at a recent event that can reverse the trend-- stay away!

3) Making use of the wrong information - As stated earlier, don't follow the headlines, follow the trend lines. Don't trade on anonymous tips. Take time to study the market and not just listen to locker room talk. Don't just act on what you receive from the media, it can be misleading sometimes. Instead, consider all factors that can affect your stocks of interest.

4) Hunger for more profit- Stock investment is not a gamble; it is a cautious endeavor -though fraught with risks. Avoid greediness at all time, it is dangerous because it will not allow you to dump a stock when you should because you are waiting endlessly for the price to shoot high into the heavens. Greed can likewise make you buy too early because you want to outsmart other investors.

STOCK INVESTMENT SECTORS

WHY A COMPANY ISSUES STOCK?

Have you ever asked yourself why should a company decide to sell its shares? Selling shares of its stock on the open market? Why not just limit ownership in the company to a few wealthy investors and keep complete control over its operations and the makeup of its board of directors? One of the main reason for doing this is to access and gain more investment money.

A company would decide to give up the control of its private ownership to raise money for research and development, new products, entry into new markets, financial growth, or acquiring competitors. An additional advantage for companies who issue stock is the low cost of using it to obtain capital. Selling stock is like an interest-free loan for a company. The stock market provides a ready-made vehicle for a company to go out and get additional funds when it wants to grow.

INITIAL PUBLIC OFFERINGS (IPO)

I know you may have heard of the IPO, the abbreviation of the Initial Public Offerings. When a company issues stock for the first time, this is called an initial public offering, or IPO. The IPO is the signal event that a company has gone from private to public ownership.

This is one way that a company can raise money from different individuals to expand further its operations.

AREAS TO INVEST FROM

Sector Investing - Stock sector investing is where you aim at buying stocks in one industry. Sector investment comes with advantages; you are able to evaluate the opportunities and risks of a stock if you know how other stocks in the same sector behave.

Here is a list of the major sectors:

1) Consumer discretionary - companies that make non-necessary goods, including retail, media, hotels, luxury items, cars, leisure and clothing

2) Consumer staples - companies that make things people will buy no matter what, including food, beverages, personal items, and cigarettes

3) Energy - fuel production companies, including oil and gas, renewables, and the products, equipment, and services that support these industries

4) Financial services - all financial companies, including insurance, banking, capital markets, trusts, credit cards and loans, and real estate (real estate is sometimes classified in its own sector)

5) Healthcare - hospitals, doctors, medical equipment, pharmaceuticals, biotech, and health and science research equipment and services

6) Industrial - anything related to manufacturing and shipping material goods, including aerospace, machinery, railroads, construction, engineering, airlines, and logistics

7) Materials - producers and extractors of raw materials for manufacturing, companies that extract or produce the raw materials, including chemicals, mining, forest products, packaging and construction materials

8) Technology - computers, software, hardware, telecommunications services and equipment, semiconductors, IT and wireless services, the internet, and office electronics. (Telecommunications is sometimes classified in its own sector.)

9) Utilities - companies involved in electrical and gas utilities, as well as power producers and energy traders.

HOW TO GAIN MONEY FROM STOCK INVESTMENT

1) DIVIDENDS

What does this term "Dividends" mean to you when it comes to stock exchange? A dividend is an agreement with a company whose stock you own to pay you a portion of its profits at a certain interval, usually quarterly. You will not find dividends from all companies, actually, those ones that do tend to be older, more stable and whose stock prices don't fluctuate as much as newer or smaller companies that do provide dividends. Growth investors look for low prices on these companies' stocks, while those who invest for income see buying stock in these companies as simply the cost of entry for receiving their dividend pay-out. These two approaches aren't mutually exclusive.

If you sell the stock in a company that pays dividends, you probably won't make a huge profit. But why would you sell if you're getting a cash pay-out every quarter?

Dividend investing means you're actually getting paid to own the stock, not just when you sell. That's why dividend investment is called "investing for income."

Things to look for when you do the evaluation risk:

1) Has the company paid out a steady or increasing dividend every year for at least the past decade?

2) Did the company actually make a profit each year it paid dividends? You want to invest in a company that's planning on liquidating.

3) Is there any emerging technology that would make the company obsolete?

4) Is the company's dividend yield too high? If the yield is high because the share price is low, then you should want to know why their stock is so cheap. It might be a great deal, but it might also have lost value for a good reason.

Beyond this basic screening process, research on a company can be as in-depth as you like, depending on your tolerance for risk and the amount of money you're going to invest. As you build skill and confidence, try to construct your own research strategy that you enjoy using, one that works for your needs.

How to Buy Dividend Stocks

You have come to a decision that you want to buy Dividends stocks after some thorough research and set a budget for your investment activities.

Your next move is to find a brokerage and open an account. Deposit at least the required minimum of cash, or however much money you plan to invest.

From here, buying and selling is simple: communicate with your broker and specify the number of shares you want for each company you are investing in. If you want to sell, the process is the same. You will want to be careful of running up brokerage fees each time you buy and sell, so make sure you plan your activities in advance before you make that phone call or log in to your brokerage website. Be sure to learn the difference between a cash account and a margin account.

2) COMPOUNDING

Compounding is another way that your stock investments make money for you. To realize the benefit of compounding, you take the profit from your initial investment and add it to that investment, instead of cashing it out and spending it.

Now you're earning interest, capital gains, or dividends on a larger chunk of money. When you profit from this sum, you roll the profits back in and make your investment even larger. Over time, your profit grows to an amount far higher than what you would have made from your initial investment alone.

If your investment portfolio includes stock in companies that pay dividends, then compounding is your secret weapon. Dividend investing goes hand in hand with compounding, thanks to special reinvestment plans aimed at dividend investors, called dividend reinvestment plans. A DRIP allows you to buy a single share, or even a fraction of a share, of a dividend-paying company, receive whatever dividend amount you're entitled to, and reinvest it in the company. Best of all, DRIPs don't require you to pay a brokerage fee.

DRIPs reinvest your dividends for you, so you're continually feeding your profit into an ever-higher investment and earning more dividends every quarter. This is truly investing for income.

MARKET CAPITALIZATION

A stock's market capitalization, or market cap for short, is the total dollar value of all the company's outstanding shares.

Investors use a formula called market capitalization (market cap for short) to determine size. The formula is:

Current price of a single share X number of shares available on the market

For example, a company whose stock price is $350 per share and has issued 20 million shares would have a market cap of $7 billion.

Companies can be classified according to their market cap. The cutoff figures vary, but the rule of thumb is:

1) $50 million or less (nano cap)

2) $50 million to $300 million (small cap)

3) $300 million to $2 billion (small cap)

4) $2 to $10 billion (mid cap)

5) $10 billion or more (large cap or blue chip stocks)

Some investors only buy stocks at one capitalization level, usually large cap.

There's a persistent belief in the financial press and among some investors and financial advisors that a big company means small risk but this doesn't mean that the size is bulletproof protection from losing money in the stock market. Precaution should be taken when undertaking any business investment.

The other thing to remember is that phrases like "small cap" and "big cap" are relative terms. The market today is much larger and is dominated by a list of big players that dwarf smaller companies in their sheer size and shares of available investment capital. The fact that these giants are so large does not necessarily mean that small-cap companies are undercapitalized.

Penny stocks - Some (but not all) nano-cap stocks are penny stocks, and although the idea of stumbling onto a bargain for pennies per share and watching it grow into an empire is appealing, the way these stocks are sold is just too risky.

For one thing, the SEC disclosure rules for penny stocks are less strict than for larger companies. Often times, penny stocks are issued as an IPO because an insolvent company wants to dump its liabilities onto unsuspecting shareholders. Penny stock brokers are complicit in the scheme, and if you buy even one of these stocks, they'll hound you at all hours of the day and night trying to get you to buy more. These people have a reputation as sharks for a reason.

STOCK MARKET TIMELINES

You may have heard of these two markets mentioned on the TVs, the Bear and Bull markets. It means that the stock market operates in two typical cycles:

Bear market - In a bear market, there is a decline in stocks prices across the market. In this case, you as the investor will lose money.

Bull market – In a bull market, there is an increase in stock prices across the market. In this case, it is the opportune moment for you to maybe sell the stock. Investors take more risk and buy more stocks.

However, during a bear market, you can grab the chance and value it as a great investment opportunity. Think about it this way, bear market stock prices are low. The fear among growth investors is that in a bear market, stock prices will just keep going down and they'll lose money even if they buy at rock bottom prices. Okay, I know you both want to have income and growth, right? Is the time to buy stocks at the lowest possible price and collect the dividends while waiting for an upturn in the market? Yes.

STOCK ANALYSIS

FUNDAMENTAL ANALYSIS

When picking stocks as a new investor, you need to analyze the market well. The analysis tends to fall into two different categories: fundamental or technical but we will take a good look at fundamentals which will work best for you.

Fundamental Analysis

This method consists of measuring the value of an investment by studying all of the factors that could affect it now or in the future. Fundamental analysis is the most mainstream method. As the name implies, this method studies the "fundamentals" of a security, be it a company or a mutual fund or a bond. The investor looks at the various metrics that indicate the health of the company before purchasing its stock.

Fundamental analysts study metrics like income, expenses, profit-and-loss, assets and liabilities, and anything related to the management and overall financial health of the investment. They also study larger financial conditions such as the state of the national and international economy, and conditions within the particular industry where the investment operates.

Financial Statements

You need to familiarize yourself with this type of document. The documents contain the financial records of a company over a period of time. It is important because it shows the status of a company. It reflects profit, growth, and assets. As an investor, you should study well the financial statements of companies to help make decisions on investments.

As a beginner, it is wise to take a look at company's financial statements to help make great investment decisions. The ratios are created by calculating the relationship between items on the financial statement with each other and/or outside forces.

A few items that I would suggest looking at:

1. Company PE ratio: The PE ratio is the price to earnings ratio for the company. A low PE ratio implies that the stock is undervalued and is a good buy. A high PE ratio implies that the stock is either overvalued or is a growth stock. One good way to determine whether the company PE ratio is good is to check the industry average PE ratio. If it is below the PE ratio, it is a good buy.

2. Debt to Asset Ratio: The Debt to Asset Ratio is a good indicator of the financial liabilities of a company. If a company has a high debt to asset ratio, check if the debt is short term or long term debt. If most of the debt is long term debt, do not rule out a buy. I would keep this as a "watch" stock.

3. Current Ratio: It is a ratio of current assets to liabilities. It is a good way to access the future of a company. If the current ratio of a company is less than 1, it means that the liabilities outweigh the assets. It may not be a good buy, unless the company is waiting for more revenue to come in. If it is a lot smaller than 1, there is a good chance of it going bankrupt. If the current ratio is greater than 3, then the company has a lot more assets than liabilities; and is a good indicator that the assets may not be utilized efficiently. This could indicate good financial standing, but low ambition and low potential for growth in the long term.

You can get information on the above ratios and many others using several online resources. The one I prefer is GuruFocus.

GETTING STARTED

Before investing in the stock market, you should know what you want and why you want it. This requires gathering substantial information to help you in deciding.

To succeed in the stock market, you need the following:

1) Understanding the reason why you want to invest - Are you buying stocks for appreciation (capital gains) or income (dividends)?

2) A good understanding of economics and economic factors that affect stock values.

3) A good knowledge of the company you are considering investing in - For instance, is the company profitable? A thorough background company research is in order.

4) Choosing the right industry to invest in. Some small companies in a fast moving industry bring good returns.

5) Identifying trends and megatrends. Know how to study market indicators for a period of time and identify the patterns and trends.

6) Understanding of how events around the world affect the industry, the company and subsequently the stock itself.

7) Defining your investment strategy - Higher risk, but higher reward? Or you want to play it safer?

After learning some basics on the stock exchange market, it is time to start making money. Well, in this chapter, you will learn the right time to buy and sell stocks.

Getting into stocks is not a difficult process. You simply need to choose the broker that you want to use and pick the right stocks and get started. You can easily transfer money and as long as you make some good decisions and don't jump ship all of the time (remember those broker fees for trades as well), you will see success and make some great money! You can follow the following steps as a novice.

Open a Brokerage Account and choosing a broker

The first thing that you will need to do in order to purchase stocks is to open up your account. You will need to find a discount broker and then sign up online to have stocks. Take a look at the different fees that the broker is going to charge.

A broker is a licensed professional who agrees to keep your money in an account and invest it according to your wishes, for a fee.

Some will have a lot higher fees compared to others and you could be losing money if you don't do your research. On the other hand, these expensive brokers may have value added services you won't find on lower tier brokerage firms. There are two types of brokers:

Full-Service Brokers - Full-service brokerage firms tout services that the discount brokers don't offer. The most common of these is extensive investment advice and financial forecasting using teams of analysts and economic experts.

Discount Brokers - Discount brokers manage your funds but don't provide advice. They work at a lower overhead than full-service brokers, so they charge far less.

Choosing a discount broker will depend on whether you want to do business with an office in your location, or conduct your trades online. Although their fees are generally reasonable, be sure to inquire closely about what exactly you'll be paying for, how much, and how often.

A couple of good brokerage accounts that I have used before are Charles Schwab and E-Trade.

Trading Simulators on the Web

Trading simulator websites are an excellent way to get a feel for how the stock market works and how stock values can change. They allow you to create your own investment account with the stock picks of your choice. Most of them are free to join. The simulator delivers a daily report for each stock and an aggregated report for your portfolio, so you can see how your simulated investment is doing. Google Finance is a great trade simulator.

Fund Your Account

Now that the account is set up, you will need to put some money into the account.

This is pretty easy to do as you just choose the right amount you want to use and either send in a check or transfer right from your bank account. The check will take a bit longer but most brokers will be fine in using it.

Select Your Stocks

Once you have your money in the account, it is time to figure out which stocks you would like to procure. If you are doing this with a financial advisor, they will be able to look at your goals and help you find the right stocks to make money with. They can pick out a few options, watch the trends for you, and help you make some important decisions to get the best profit. If you are doing it on your own, you will need to be proactive and watch the different stocks to make sure you are picking the right ones to make a profit.

Understanding Transaction Costs

A key term or set of terms to understand before you call or click on your brokerage account is bid-ask spread. This affects the price at which you will be able to buy shares of a stock you want to add to your portfolio and therefore your portfolio's total return on your investment:

1) Bid - The highest price that you, the buyer, are willing to pay for a share.

2) Ask - The lowest price at which the seller is willing to sell you that share.

3) Bid-Ask Spread -The difference between the bid and the ask.

The spread can vary, depending on how often a share is traded. Currency assets and large-company stocks change hands on a daily basis, so their spread is very low; while stocks with fewer shares or a lower trading volume may have a higher spread.

The recipient of the spread amount is the market maker, sometimes called a specialist, who pockets the difference between the bid and the ask as profit. The market maker plays a vital role in the marketplace by keeping stocks liquid at all times, ready to be bought and sold. Generally, the higher the demand for a stock, the lower the spread, since more market makers are needed to handle the demand, so competition increases among them.

Remember that the bid-ask spread is separate from your broker's commissions and fees, which are another cost. Added up together, they represent your total transaction costs for your stock purchase. You need to be aware of these costs and make sure they stay at a level you can accept, but they're a fact of life and a cost of doing business in the market. When you purchase a stock at the ask price, its value in your portfolio is actually the bid price, since the difference goes to the maker.

Before you start wringing your hands in despair over losing money right away, remember that the spread is only a loss if you plan to turn around and sell your shares right away. Since the whole point of buying a stock is to hold it long enough to make money through capital appreciation and/or dividends, you should be able to absorb your transaction costs as your portfolio increases in value.

Keeping Brokerage Fees Under Control

Some brokerages charge a monthly fee, while others charge a fee per transaction. If you're an active investor who makes frequent trades, look for monthly fees. Passive investors should opt for a fee per transaction agreement while looking closely for minimum monthly trade requirements.

In either case, you need to look at the fee agreements very carefully before you sign up and make sure your broker answers your questions. Any signs of evasion or hard-sell tactics are good reasons to take your business elsewhere.

Placing an Order

Ready to buy or sell? It's time to learn about the types of orders you, as an individual investor, can place with your broker. Keep in mind that whether you are buying or selling a stock, both transactions are called orders in the lingo of the marketplace because you're giving your broker instructions. There several different types of orders in the stock market, however, we are going to discuss a few of them below.

1) **Market Order** - This tells your broker to immediately buy or sell a stock at the best price currently available. Since you haven't placed a limit on the price or the time in which the order can be carried out, these orders are considered unrestricted. That means a lower-volume stock could have a much higher ask price than

the current market price displayed on your stock chart, resulting in considerable sticker shock when you see the spread you just paid for. With higher-volume, in-demand stocks, a market order is safer and can result in some savings on broker commissions since there is little work involved.

2) **Limit Order** - Here you tell your broker to stick to a certain price limit and even time. For instance, when you set a limit of $30 per share, then your broker will only buy this stock for you if the ask price is $30 or less; and he will only sell it for you at a bid of $30 or more.

Broker commissions on limit orders and other orders with time and price constraints tend to be higher than for market orders.

3) **Stop Order** - Also known as a stop-loss order, this sets a predetermined entry point for a buy or an exit point for a sale. If and when the stock reaches this point, your order converts to a market order. The intent of a stop order is to lock in your profit and protect yourself from loss, but it doesn't always work that way. Your entry or exit point is only a benchmark. For example, if the price dips lower than your exit point, the sale will still execute, at a lower price than you intended. One way to avoid this is to place a stop limit order in- stead, which allows you to cut off the sale if it exceeds the range you specify.

4) **Trailing Stop Order** - This allows you to track the direction of a stock's price automatically and sell if its price goes down by more than a certain percentage compared to the price you paid for it. For example, if bought a stock at $10; and see it at $30; you can do a stop order at $30 to lock in your $20 profit. But you can also do a trailing stop at $25. This means that if the stock falls to $25, it will sell. But if the stock goes to $45; the new stop is at $40 ($5 below maximum). The stop value keeps increasing until it is sold. It is a great way of maximizing profits by riding market momentum.

Diversify

If you are a beginner, you should diversify your portfolio a bit. It is never a good idea to put all of your money in just one stock. Buy different stocks from different industries. Diversifying your portfolio limits your risk. Sure, you could make a lot of money if the stock does well, but if it does poorly, you could end up losing it all in one swoop.

So pick at least two or three stocks to divide your money in. This way, if one stock does poorly, you still have the others to hold you up and making you money.

DIFFERENT TYPES OF TRADING PROCESS

1) Day Trading

Day trading is a type of investing where you will buy and then sell your stocks all on the same day. The trading will need to close before the market has closed down for the day. If you are a trader who goes in on this day trading, you are called an active trader. This is a good option if you would like the ability to make money quickly and you are able to take fast action while making decisions right away.

This is a tough kind of trading and it is not recommended for those who are just getting into the stock market. Most stocks are going to see growth over time, but if you are following the stock for just a day, you may see a dramatic decrease during this time. As a day trader, you need to have a good understanding of how the market works and be able to recognize trends enough to stay on top of it all.

There are a few different methods that you can use when going with day trading. These methods include:

a) **Arbitrage** - This can be helpful in capturing slight changes in the price. When there are differences in prices of a stock which is located in two different places, the trader would pick the one that is lower priced and then sells it on the higher priced market. For this one, you will look at two or more places for the stock. If they are all the same price, it doesn't make sense to purchase it. But if you can find it for a lower price, you would make the purchase and sell it on the other site right away for a higher price to make a profit.

b) **Market Making** - The stock exchanges are going to appoint the market makers and will be the ones who provide `ask and bid' rates to the brokers when buying and selling stocks on the big exchange sites.

c) **Momentum day trading** - This is a type of stock trading where a certain trade is made while the stock is trending in movement and then the trade will close down at the end of the market day.

d) **Pattern trading** - As the price of the stock goes up and down, you will start to notice a pattern over time and can even see them on the charts. You will be able to use pattern trading to determine if your day stock is going up or down so you can act accordingly.

e) **Scalping** - This method involves getting small profits quickly from hundreds of trades during the day. You will use the 'ask and bid' differences given to you and make a ton of trades all day long. You will not make a ton of money off each stock, but overall, with so many trades, you are going to see a profit.

f) **Price Action Trading** - With this method, you will only consider the price actions.

g) You will need to decide on a time period from 1 to 60 minutes, and then you will trade it during that day. You will simply look at the open, high, low, and then close during that time period to make money.

h) **Rebate trading** - This is a day trading method where you will be paid by your service provided for buying and selling stocks.

i) **News Playing** - This is a method where you will follow the news releases that show up during the day. You will decide to buy and sell based on these news releases and it is going to be closed within one day as well. For example, you hear that Apple is releasing a new iPhone and decide to buy Apple shares on the expectation that it is going to appreciate in value.

2) Short Term Trading

This is similar to day trading, but you are going to have more than a day to get it done. It is usually between two days and a few weeks for trading. For this type, you will purchase a stock and then hold onto it for a day up to two weeks. After this time, you will sell it again, hopefully for a nice profit. This kind of trade is entered when you create a sell position, which will then be covered later on. Pattern trading and swig trading are good examples of how this works.

3) Medium Trading

This is where we get into the longer term trading options for the stock market. This is usually going to last anywhere from a few weeks to a few months. The trend here is followed with tailoring any stop loss. Swing trading and Elliot wave trading are good to use when you want to stick with medium trading. This one is a good option if you would like to follow the trends a bit more but don't want to work with the stocks for too long.

4) Long Term Trading

This kind of trading can last anywhere from a few months to many years. If you have a retirement account, you are probably playing with long term trading because the stocks are going to basically stay put for a long time to come. You will see a lot less risk with this option because you have time to go through the different progressions of the stock and will generally earn a good profit.

All stocks go through periods of ups and downs. That is just how business works. If you are sticking with some of the shorter term trading options listed above, you may be hit with some of the downturns of a particular stock without much time to come back when the stock prices go back up. With long term investing, you may lose some money temporarily, but you can also see big gains in your money. When you stick with a stock for the long term, you are generally going to come out way ahead than you started.

Talk to your financial advisor about going with a longer term option if this seems like it would fit your overall goals.

THE RIGHT TIME TO BUY STOCKS

1) When a Company's Stock is undervalued - When you know the stock price of a company is lower than its book value, there is huge potential for growth in the future. This is like the opposite of a bubble, where- by a company's stock is trading higher than its real value. If you notice that a company's stock is undervalued, buy and watch patiently as market forces drive the price up in the future. You can know this from careful study of the company and analysis of its financial statement. If you are doing short term investment, you may not be able to do this.

2) When a Company is growing - If you have seen remarkable recent growth in a company's size, profit and stability you need to buy fast. Remember, many other investors are studying the company just as you are doing. If they start buying before you, the price will start increasing. That is why you need to start investing early, but not too early. To minimize risk, you can have a predetermined threshold.

3) When Stock Price Rises to Your "Buy Price" - Since you cannot always predict accurately if a stock's price will continue to rise indefinitely or fall soon, you need to set up a range of value at which you buy a stock.

For instance, if the stock price shows a rise of 5% within a week (from $20 to $21), and you can relate the increase to an increase in the company's growth; you can buy it in the second week after it rises from $21 to 22$

4) When a Company is Strong - Very big and strong companies are known as blue chips. The reason why the prices of blue chip stocks keep rising is because people keep buying them and people keep buying them because they trust that they are stable. These companies have weathered the storms in the past and have come out stronger. Therefore, investors believe they will show resilience. If you are investing in the long term and interested in security, buy into a strong company and watch your investment grow steadily into the future.

THE RIGHT TIME TO SELL STOCK

1) In case you realize you have made a mistake - If you suddenly discover that you made a mistake while purchasing a stock, you need to sell it quickly. If you realize that while buying the stock you made an error in judgment or you have bought it for the wrong reasons, you need to sell it fast. It is a bad stock. The key to

successful investing is to rely on data, strategy and analysis and not on your emotional swings. If the analysis you carried out before buying is flawed, you will only make more mistakes if you hold on to it because you do not have control over it. The stock price may go up after you sell, but you won't be able to predict correctly, what will happen to it in the future. It is true that everyone makes mistakes but learning from a mistake that costs you a 10% loss on your investment could be one of the best investment decisions you could make.

2) When there is a Significant Rise - It is true that nobody can totally predict the market. Therefore, you may never know when a stock has reached its highest or lowest value. When a stock you bought for less is appreciating fast and it gets to the point you are comfortable with selling it.

To make it easier, always plan from the outset, the limit of appreciation; that is the highest value the stock will get to before you sell. For instance, you can say that for every 5% increase in the value of a certain stock, you will sell 25% of your stocks.

3) Dramatic company changes - This usually applies to long term investments. We usually put our money in certain companies because they have certain qualities that guarantee security, growth and profit. These qualities may include stability, strong

financial records and large market cap. When these things begin to change, it is time to review your investments.

Sometimes the change is not significant enough to make you sell, but sometimes it is. For instance if you bought stocks into a certain company due to its long-term stability, strength, size and market cap and the company is suddenly acquired? You will be the one to review your investment. If the new owner starts laying off workers and there is a lot of negative publicity, or the company starts losing money? It is time to sell. Note that other investors in the company are studying the same things as you, and if they begin to sell before you-you will start noticing a drop in the stock prices. Sell immediately, before you start incurring a loss. Follow your guts, but also be cautious.

If you think the company can still bounce back, you may not want sell all your shares. You can retain a small share for future trading. Another reason to sell is bankruptcy. If this happens, sell all your stocks immediately, without looking back.

4) When there is a Noticeable Dip in Stock Price - There is no reason to keep a losing stock. When you notice that your stock is losing value rapidly, sell it before it falls below the price you bought it. If you bought it at a higher price and you have already made a loss - sell it immediately before your loss hits 10% so that your loss doesn't multiply. However, if other factors point to the ability of the company stocks to rebound or the market is in a

bullish trend, you may retain a few stocks; let's say in the 30% range.

FREQUENTLY ASKED QUESTIONS

1) How do I start investing in stocks?

Open an investment account with a broker. While a few hundred companies allow you to buy your first share of stock directly from them, most companies trade their shares only on stock exchanges or through dealer networks. A brokerage account will give you access to thousands of stocks and will make the account setup process easy.

2) How much money do I need to start investing in stocks?

You may fear to invest in stocks because of huge money to invest, actually, you can invest with as little as $1,000.

3) How do I know which stocks to buy?

Below, we are going to discuss the tricks and tips to evaluating which stocks to buy:

Value – As a novice, you shouldn't mess around with pricey hyper growth stocks. Before you buy, consider the stock's key valuation ratios.

Growth - Even the cheapest stock isn't worth buying if the company can't increase its profits. Rising sales, profits, and cash flow suggest the company's products sell well enough to increase its penetration of the market.

Profitability – A well-managed company can maintain its profit margins while still growing. As an investor, you should target stocks with stable or rising profitability.

News – Gather and get all the information concerning the stock market, what kind of headlines does the stock generate? Both good news and bad news can affect a stock's price before any changes trickle down to the income statement or balance sheet.

4) How do I know when to sell a stock?

Even with the prolific investors, they will find the sell decision tougher than the buy decision because they only buy stocks they like. Once you purchase a stock you enjoy owning, you may find it difficult to part with the investment.

There is no straight answer to this question. It depends on your personal goals. I recommend a lower and upper threshold for each stock pre-set before you buy the stock. If the stock reaches upper or lower threshold, you should sell or buy the stock. This way, you can leave your emotions behind when you make this important decision.

5) How do I track my portfolio?

In the modern world today, the internet has made the stock market exchange easier with good provision of information in a timely fashion. These days, the Internet simply offers more information, and provides the pricing and trading data.

You can check out the performance of your stocks on your discount broker's website. While each broker does the job a little differently, they should all show you the value of your stock positions and allow you to view the stocks' history; how they have moved since you purchased them.

Charles Schwab and E-Trade are ones that I would recommend in the US.

6) Do I need a broker?

A broker will help you with good investment decisions, commit more time to your investments and analyze the stock numbers comfortably.

CONCLUSION

It is my hope that after reading this book, you will be able to make one step further and venture into the world of stock investment easily. It is true that the world of stocks investment is somewhat complicated but a good follow-up on these guidelines will erase the sharp ranges ahead of you. It is simple for those who enter it with the right knowledge while it is complicated for those who don't have the requisite knowledge. In addition to saving and making sure you have enough money for your everyday expenses, planning for long-term objectives such as retirement, education or a large purchase is essential. It is time to get started, what are you waiting for? The above tricks and techniques are the primary factors that will help you make the first step into the fire. Always remember that hard-work and perseverance pay off.

Good Luck!

www.ingramcontent.com/pod-product-compliance
Ingram Content Group UK Ltd.
Pitfield, Milton Keynes, MK11 3LW, UK
UKHW021259180426
11947UKWH00015B/924